Not a Silent Night
Mary Looks Back to Bethlehem

Youth Leader Guide

Not a Silent Night
Mary Looks Back to Bethlehem

Book
978-1-426-77184-2
978-1-426-79396-7 eBook
978-1-630-88295-2 Large Print

DVD
978-1-426-77185-9

Leader Guide
978-1-426-77199-6
978-1-630-88035-4 eBook

Youth Study Book
978-1-501-81569-0
978-1-501-81570-6 eBook

Youth Leader Guide
978-1-501-81571-3
978-1-501-81572-0 eBook

For more information, visit www.AdamHamilton.org.

Also by Adam Hamilton

24 Hours That Changed the World

Christianity and World Religions

Christianity's Family Tree

Confronting the Controversies

Enough

Final Words from the Cross

Forgiveness

Leading Beyond the Walls

Love to Stay

Making Sense of the Bible

Revival

Seeing Gray in a World of Black and White

Selling Swimsuits in the Arctic

The Call

The Journey

The Way

Unleashing the Word

When Christians Get It Wrong

Why?

ADAM HAMILTON

NOT A
SILENT NIGHT

MARY LOOKS BACK TO BETHLEHEM

Youth Leader Guide
by Mike Poteet

(Consists of Leader Helps + Youth Study Book)

Abingdon Press / Nashville

NOT A SILENT NIGHT:
MARY LOOKS BACK AT BETHLEHEM

YOUTH LEADER GUIDE
by Mike Poteet

15 16 17 18 19 20 21 22 23 24—10 9 8 7 6 5 4 3 2 1
MANUFACTURED IN THE UNITED STATES OF AMERICA

CONTENTS

Leader Helps

Introduction

Welcome to the Youth Leader Guide for the *Not a Silent Night* study program.

Adam Hamilton's book *Not a Silent Night* follows the life of Jesus through the eyes of his mother, Mary. As the introduction to the Youth Study Book emphasizes, Mary was a thoughtful and contemplative person. In keeping with her character, this youth study doesn't contain high-energy icebreakers, games, skits, or challenges. All those elements of youth ministry have their place, but this resource seeks to foster a different kind of experience—one that will encourage youth to treasure and ponder God's Word in their hearts, as Mary did (see Luke 2:19, 51).

Through Scripture, prayer, the written word, music, visual art, crafts, and even food, this study will help you create time and space for youth to reflect, in the midst of a busy holiday season full of distractions, on Jesus' significance for them—not just as the baby of Bethlehem, but as one who grew as they are growing, who lived a fully human life in obedience to God, and who died and was raised in order to give new and everlasting life.

About This Youth Leader Guide

As you may have noticed on the title page and in the contents, this Youth Leader Guide consists of two parts: Leader Helps and Youth Study Book.

This first part of the guide, Leader Helps, gives you as leader the information and support you'll need to facilitate a successful study with your group. The second part of the guide, Youth Study Book, reproduces in full the participant book, allowing you—literally—to be on the same page as the group.

In the Leader Helps, you'll find descriptions of nine activities, which correspond to the nine activities in each chapter of the Youth Study Book:

- Lighting the Advent Candles
- Scripture Focus
- Mary Ponders
- Reading for Reflection
- Meditating with Art
- Meditating with Music
- *Lectio Divina*
- Ponder Giving This Present
- This Week, Wonder With God About . . .

In addition, the Leader Helps include a section of suggested Crafts and Recipes that you can use to extend and enhance your sessions.

Please refer to this format as you read the Leader Helps, so you'll have a sense of how you want and need to plan your sessions to best serve the youth with whom you minister. You may or may not want or be able to use all the activities every time. Also, please note that the instructions and tips in the Leader Helps generally apply to all four of the full sessions; however, where appropriate, information specific to certain sessions appears.

Activities

LIGHTING THE ADVENT CANDLES
Responsive reading to accompany candle-lighting

In the Youth Study Book, each session begins with a litany or responsive reading, a Christmas carol, and a prayer. Starting each group session with the litany will help establish a contemplative mood for reading, reflection, and prayer. It will also connect your study with the larger church's observance of the Advent season.

Choose a place in your meeting space to be a worship center. Arrange your Advent candles on the floor or on a small table: four smaller candles surrounding a larger, white candle in the center (symbolizing Christ, the Light of the World). Customary colors for Advent candles are purple (the color of royalty, since we are waiting to celebrate the birth of the King of Kings; also a color of repentance, since we prepare for his coming again as Judge) and blue (adopted more recently in some traditions as a color of hope, and to distinguish Advent from Lent, which also uses purple). Some traditions use a rose or pink candle on the Third Sunday of Advent to represent anticipation of Christmas joy. Follow your church's customs, and, if meeting in a church building, check with leadership about whether you should use wax or electric candles. (Some church insurance policies restrict the use of open flames.)

You can recruit up to five youth to lead each week's printed litany as a responsive reading, assigning a different portion of the litany to each: the greeting, the Old Testament text, the words of Jesus, the identification of the candle(s) being lit, and the prayer. Everyone should read together the words in bold, and sing or recite together the carol verses. In a larger group, choose as many different readers over the course of the sessions as possible.

SCRIPTURE FOCUS
Main Bible passage to be studied each week

The Youth Study Book also includes a Scripture for each session. Bible chapter and verse numbers have been removed to encourage a more direct encounter with the text. Recruit one or more strong readers to read aloud this Scripture as other youth follow along silently.

After the Scripture reading, encourage youth to ask questions about the text; you might start discussion by asking your own questions. The point is not necessarily to answer all the questions, but to allow time and space for asking them.

You might consider writing the questions on newsprint or markerboard so youth can keep them in mind as the session continues, or assign interested youth to research the questions during the coming week and report their findings to the group at the next session.

MARY PONDERS
Dramatic monologue by Mary

One of the most unique and moving features of the Youth Study Book is the dramatic monologues by Mary. Recruit a strong female reader (from inside or outside the group) to read aloud each session's monologue with expression and attention to meaning. If possible, recruit someone with an interest in drama and theater. Make sure she has adequate time to read and prepare each week's monologue. Consider audio or video recording of the monologues, either in advance or during the performance, so that others in your congregation might listen to or watch them as well. Your reader may want to devise a costume, but it is not necessary.

When recruiting your reader, note that Mary's age changes from session to session:

- In the monologue for Session One, Mary is 45–50 years old.
- In the monologues for Sessions Two and Four (as well as the additional monologue in Chapter 5), Mary is a teenager.
- In the monologue for Session Three, Mary is in her mid-twenties.

Certainly, actors need not be the same age as the characters they portray, but you may want to recruit women of these ages for the various sessions in order to enhance participants' experiences.

Although each session's monologue text is printed in the book, encourage youth to shut their books and actively watch and listen to each session's performance. After each monologue, invite reactions and discuss any new insights or questions the monologue raises; youth can refer to the text at this point. (Though youth can share positive feedback with the performer, avoid letting this portion of the session become a theater review. Keep the group focused on content.)

If you are unable to recruit performers, allow time for youth to read the monologue as part of your session.

READING FOR REFLECTION
Devotional essay expanding on themes from each session's Scripture

Participants will find a devotional essay in each session of their book. Either allow time for youth to read the session's devotional essay, or ask them to read it prior to the session and then review highlights during your group meeting. Use the questions below to help start discussion.

Session One

- So far this holiday season, where and how have you seen Mary depicted? How do these depictions compare with the way you usually think about Mary?
- How would you describe Mary's prominence in your own congregation's worship life?
- Paul used the image of a victor's crown as a metaphor for eternal life. What image(s) of eternal life appeal to you, and why?
- If you had been in the early Christian community with Mary, what would you have wanted to ask her?
- Talk about a time when you feel you have been told, "Do whatever [Jesus] tells you." What did you do? What happened?
- How are you waiting for Jesus without "just waiting around"?

Session Two

- What's the strangest crèche you've ever seen?
- In our culture, why do you think so many versions of the Christmas story leave out its darker, more dangerous aspects, such as King Herod's actions and Simeon's prophecy?
- How would you answer if someone asked whether Jesus had to die on the cross?
- Do you find it more meaningful to think about Jesus saving us from our sins (the individual wrongs we commit), or from sin (the power opposed to God's will)? Why?
- When have you experienced the church acting most like the family Jesus makes it?
- What troubles are looming over your life this Advent? How can your brothers, sisters, mothers, and fathers in faith help you as you face them?

Session Three

- How do you react when people ask what you want to do with your life?
- How have your thoughts about what do with your life changed since you were a child?
- What would you most like to know about Jesus' teenage years?
- What are you already doing to be "in your Father's house" and "about your Father's business"? What would you like to do?
- Talk with someone else in your group about ways each of you can imagine God using the other person to glorify God and serve your neighbors.

Session Four

- How would you have reacted if you had been in the audience that heard the graduation speaker say, "You're not special"?
- How special do you think Mary was? Why?
- Consider this statement from the essay: "A big part of the meaning of Christmas is that it's *precisely* the people who don't matter to the world who matter the most to God." Do you agree? Why or why not?
- What do you do to pay attention to the "humble" people whom others overlook?
- If Mary were singing the Magnificat at your school, whom would she say God will pull down and lift up? Why?

MEDITATING WITH ART
Using visual images as a tool for prayer and meditation

Remind the group that meditating or praying with art is a different way of looking at art. The object is not to critique the artwork, but to view it as something through which the Holy Spirit might be speaking to us.

For each session, encourage youth to sit comfortably and quietly, and to spend several minutes gazing at the art, allowing their attention to be drawn to various details. You could play quiet, instrumental background music during the meditation, or have youth meditate in silence. When you sense that sufficient time has passed, invite volunteers to talk about what details from the art drew their attention and what thoughts or feelings they had while looking at the art. Close this section of each session by asking, "What might God be calling you to do or be through this artwork?"

If you feel it would be helpful for your group to have specific questions to prompt discussion, here are some suggestions:

Session One

- Mountains often represent the meeting of the earthly and the heavenly, in our own religion and in others. What places do you associate with God?
- Some believe that the risen and ascended Jesus' footprints are still visible on the Mount of Olives. When have you "seen Jesus' footprints"—traces of Jesus' presence and work—in the world or in your life?
- As we study the art, Mary appears to be looking directly at us. What do you imagine she might say to you? Why?

Session Two

- What words would you use to describe how Mary is holding the dead Jesus?
- What do you imagine Mary is thinking or saying as she looks to heaven in this statue?

Session Three

- How would you describe the artist's depiction of Jesus?
- What might Mary and Joseph's appearance suggest about their relationship to Jesus, in this artist's interpretation?
- What do the teachers' poses suggest about their level of engagement with this conversation with Jesus? Are they all involved to the same degree?
- Where do you usually fall on the spectrum of involvement in your conversations with Jesus, through reading of Scripture and prayer?

Session Four

- How would you describe the mood of the scene in this sculpture?
- Why is the angel kneeling before Mary?

MEDITATING WITH MUSIC
Listening and responding to music inspired by Mary or Scripture

Each session contains two musical suggestions; use one or both, as time allows. In all cases, invite youth to talk about their initial reactions to the music, then use the questions printed in the book to prompt discussion. Close this part of the session by asking, "When you hear this music, what do you hear God calling you to be or do?"

LECTIO DIVINA
Learning and practicing contemplative reading of the Bible

Each session includes the ancient practice of *lectio divina* ("divine reading" or "spiritual reading"). In *lectio divina*, we read a biblical text more with the heart than with the head. In this form of Bible study, we don't try to master content but rather seek to make time and space to hear God speak through Scripture.

For each session, recruit three volunteers to read aloud the text printed in the book. Each volunteer should read at a steady pace: deliberately, but not too slowly; with attention to meaning, but avoiding "performance." (This approach is in contrast to the "Mary Ponders" monologues, which are intended to be dramatic performances.)

Explain to the group that the text will be read aloud three times. Youth who are not reading aloud should close their books; this is a discipline that involves hearing the text, not necessarily looking at it. Many specific models of *lectio divina* exist; here is a suggested method you can use.

1. During the first reading, hearers should be alert for a word, phrase, or image that captures their attention— that "sparkles" for them.
2. After the first reading, allow a minute or so of silence, then invite hearers to speak aloud, without comment or explanation, the word, phrase, or image that attracted their attention.
3. During the second reading, hearers should listen while meditating on their chosen word, phrase, or image. How does that word, phrase, or image intersect with their lives today? Why do they think this portion of the text attracted their attention?
4. After a longer silence (2–3 minutes), invite volunteers to speak aloud about the connection of their word, phrase, or image to their lives. Other participants may ask questions of clarification but should refrain from extended conversations.
5. During the third and final reading, hearers should listen while thinking about what God is calling them to be or do through this text.
6. Allow another 2–3 minutes of silence, then invite volunteers to talk about how they sense God speaking through the text. At this point, youth may engage each other in conversation.

Close this section of each session by leading a prayer, asking God to help group members follow through on whatever commitments they have sensed and talked about as a result of this meditation.

PONDER GIVING THIS PRESENT
Discussing alternative gift-giving

The Youth Study Book offers alternative gift-giving possibilities tied to each session's theme. However, you need not feel constrained by these suggestions. Your congregation or denomination may already support a ministry or charity whose mission aligns with a given session's focus, or you may have an idea all your own. The goal is to encourage youth to think this Christmas about giving gifts of money and time that will benefit others. View these suggestions as starting points only!

THIS WEEK, WONDER WITH GOD ABOUT . . .
Devotional take-away tool for participants

Encourage youth to use each week's daily Scriptures and questions as part of their personal prayer time during Advent.

Crafts and Recipes

If possible, enhance your sessions with the crafts and recipes described below. Although these should not prove especially difficult, they will take some extra time. In keeping with the program's contemplative nature, view this time as a gift. Use it as an opportunity not only to talk informally about each session's Scripture and themes, but also to develop deeper relationships in your youth ministry as participants work together on these projects.

SESSION ONE

Soda Can Crown

This craft lets youth make a version of the ancient laurel wreath, a frequent symbol of eternal life in the New Testament, out of a very modern material: an aluminum soda can.

Each participant will need an empty and dry soda can, glue, scissors, plastic headband, gold-colored paint, and a paintbrush.

1. Paint the headband and set it aside to dry.
2. Cut off the top and bottom of the soda can and discard them in a safe place. *(Note: In this step and those that follow, take care to avoid being cut on sharp edges.)*
3. Cut the can, moving straight down one side, and unroll the can to make a small, flat sheet of aluminum.
4. Cut out several aluminum "leaves," of whatever shape and size you desire.
5. Paint the leaves.
6. Once leaves and headband are completely dry, glue the leaves onto the headband, placing them as you desire.
7. When dry, your "crown" is ready to wear.

(Based on Becky Kremm's video tutorial "DIY: Laurel Headband," http://www.youtube.com/watch?v=oeeAXFnBGrE.)

Crowned Cupcakes

Continue the session's crown motif by making and decorating cupcakes that resemble regal headwear. You will need:

2 cups flour
1/2 teaspoon salt
2 teaspoons baking powder
1/2 cup softened butter
3/4 cup sugar
2 eggs
1 cup milk
vanilla frosting (optional: blue food coloring)
assorted cake decorations (sprinkles, gumdrops, "silver balls," and so on)
mixing bowls, large and small
cupcake/muffin baking tins
paper cupcake liners

1. Preheat oven to 375 degrees.
1. Put paper liners in baking tin cups.
2. In large mixing bowl, cream butter and sugar to a light, fluffy consistency.
3. Add and beat eggs, one at a time.
4. In the small bowl, mix flour, baking powder, and salt.
5. Add flour mixture to the butter-egg mixture, alternating with milk. Mix well.
6. Pour even portions of the batter into the baking tin cups and bake for about 18 minutes, or until an inserted tooth-pick comes out clean.
7. When the cupcakes are cool, add frosting—colored blue with food coloring, if desired, since blue is traditionally associated with Mary—and decorate to resemble a crown with jewels.

Yield: 20–25 cupcakes

(Cupcake recipe adapted from "Simple Vanilla Cupcakes," http://www.food.com/recipe/simple-vanilla-cupcakes-178370.)

SESSION TWO

Woven Cross

Mary endured the ugly sight of watching her child die, and in the ugliest way known in the ancient Roman world. But she, along with Jesus' other followers, would discover on the first Easter Day that God can transform even something as ugly as the cross into a thing of beauty. This craft allows youth to make their own beautiful crosses, which they can use as a focal point when praying.

You will need a block of wood at least 1/2 inch thick, nails (at least five 1-1/2-inch nails), a hammer, scissors, and yarn (one or several colors, as desired).

Hammer the nails into your block of wood to make the shape of a cross. You can either use five nails—one at each of the cross's ends and one in the center—or you can use several nails to outline a cross shape, depending on how elaborate you wish your finished product to be. Do not hammer the nails into the wood completely; make sure enough of each nail sticks out that you can easily wrap yarn around it.

1. Wrap an end of yarn around one of your nails (it doesn't matter which one) and tie a knot to secure it.
2. Wind the yarn around the rest of the nails, as few or as many times as you wish.
3. If you want to add more than one color of yarn, cut off and tie a knot in the first yarn length before starting again at step 2. You may want to push down the first layer of yarn to make room for the next.
4. When you're satisfied with your weaving, tie the yarn you're using to a nail and cut off the excess.

(Adapted from "DIY: Wall Art" at http://www.cremedelacraft.com/2012/08 /diy-wall-art-from-yarn-nails.html and "Simple String Art—Weaving an Easter Cross" at http://www.sunhatsandwellieboots.com/2015/03/simple -string-art-weaving-easter-cross.html.)

Christ Child Crepes

Many Christians in France and Belgium eat crepes on the Feast of the Presentation of the Lord (February 2), which commemorates Joseph, Mary, and baby Jesus' visit to the Temple in Jerusalem, as related in this session's focal Scripture. Why crepes? One Roman Catholic blogger suggests, "I think that the crepes look like a swaddled baby" (http://catholiccuisine .blogspot.com/2009/02/candlemas-crepes.html).

You will need:

2 eggs
1 cup flour
1/2 cup milk
1/2 cup water
2 tablespoons melted butter
1/4 teaspoon salt
whipped cream (homemade or store-bought)
fresh or thawed frozen berries
powdered sugar
whisk
large bowl
vegetable oil or baking spray
griddle or frying pan
spatula
wax paper

1. Lightly grease griddle or frying pan with vegetable oil or baking spray, and place it over medium-high heat.
2. Using the whisk, mix the eggs and flour together in a large bowl.
3. Add milk and water a little bit at a time. Keep mixing.
4. Add butter and salt. Mix until smooth.
5. Pour batter into the griddle or the pan a scant 1/4 cup at a time, tilting the surface so that the batter coats the inside surface evenly.
6. Cook for approximately 2 minutes. When the bottom is light brown, loosen the crepe with a spatula, flip it over, and cook the other side.
7. When the crepe is done, remove from griddle or pan and let cool on wax paper.
8. When cool enough to eat, add some dollops of whipped cream in the center of each crepe and roll it up, placing it on a plate with the seam side down. Top with berries and powdered sugar as desired.

Yield: 8 crepes

SESSION THREE

Memory Wire Meditation Beads

Many Roman Catholic Christians use rosaries (sometimes called "prayer beads") as an aid to prayer. The beads prompt users to recite the Apostles' Creed and to say various prayers—the Lord's Prayer, the "Hail Mary," and the Gloria Patri—and to reflect on various "mysteries," both sorrowful and joyful, in Mary's life.

As you and your youth make prayer beads as described below, you can choose how the beads will prompt your praying. You might associate certain colors with certain types of prayer—perhaps a gold bead with a prayer of praise, or a red bead with a prayer for help—or you might spell out words (for example, GRACE or LOVE) to use in your prayers. Encourage youth to make creative associations that they consider relevant and useful for their prayer lives.

You will need memory wire (with a coil of about 2 inches in diameter), memory wire shears or heavy-duty wire cutters (regular shears or other jewelry-making tools will not work on memory wire), round-nose pliers, and a variety of plastic, glass, or wood craft beads.

1. Using the memory wire shears or heavy-duty wire cutters, cut the desired length of memory wire (you will want to work with at least one full loop). Cut the wire about two inches past the end of the last loop.
2. Using the round-nose pliers, form a small loop at one end of your length of memory wire. This loop (like a knot at the end of a thread) will stop beads from slipping off.
3. String the beads onto the memory wire as you wish.
4. Leave enough memory wire at the other end to form another small loop with the round-nose pliers.

(Adapted from the video tutorial "How to Make a Memory Wire Bracelet" at https://www.youtube.com/watch?v=Hyz8alYsHul.)

Joseph's "Sawdust" Spaghetti

Many Italian Roman Catholics celebrate the Feast of St. Joseph (March 19) by eating pasta topped with bread crumbs, to remind diners of the sawdust that would have filled Joseph's carpentry shop. To make this spaghetti extra "dusty," top with grated parmesan cheese—an additional reminder of the humble circumstances in which Jesus was raised.

You will need:

uncooked spaghetti (1 lb. package)
2 heaping tablespoons minced garlic
1/4 cup olive oil
1 cup bread crumbs
water
salt
large pan
colander

1. Boil water, as much as you will need for the amount of pasta you intend to prepare.
2. Once water boils, add salt.
3. Boil desired portion of spaghetti according to package instructions.
4. Drain spaghetti. Leave it in colander and set aside.
5. Mix garlic, olive oil, and bread crumbs in pan. Stir over low heat until the bread crumbs are lightly browned.
6. Mix in the spaghetti and a dash of salt. Coat spaghetti thoroughly in bread-crumb mixture.

Yield: 4–6 servings

(Adapted from http://www.cookingwithnonna.com/italian-cuisine/easy-spaghetti-with-bread-crumbs-garlic.html.)

SESSION FOUR

Humble Candleholder

Make these humble candleholders as reminders of the
humility with which Mary agreed to be the bearer of Jesus
Christ, the Light of the World.

You will need an empty, clean, and dry glass jar (of any size);
several sheets of colored tissue paper; Mod Podge® (matte finish)
or similar glue/sealer (watered-down school glue can work); a
paintbrush or sponge brush; and a votive candle large enough to
stand unsupported inside the jar.

Be sure to check in advance to find out if you are allowed
to light a candle in your classroom. If you are not allowed to,
end the activity at step 5 and encourage youth to take the
candleholder home to use in a safe place.

1. Tear or cut the tissue paper into small pieces.
2. Paint a thin layer of Mod Podge onto a small section of
    the jar's outer surface, then cover that section with pieces
    of tissue paper. Repeat until you have covered the entire
    surface. You may wish to at least occasionally overlap
    pieces of tissue paper.
3. Slowly paint over the entire tissue-covered surface with
    another thin layer of Mod Podge.
4. Allow the jar to dry completely.
5. When your jar is dry, place the votive candle inside.
6. In a dark room, light the candle. Enjoy watching the light
    shine!

Magnificent Magnificat Cupcakes

Our program began with cupcakes in Session One, and it
ends with more cupcakes in Session Four. These cupcakes are
miniature pineapple-upside-down cakes that can remind us of

how Mary, in the Magnificat, rejoices in the way God will turn the world and its values upside down through the birth of her son.

You will need:

1 box (15.25 oz.) yellow or pineapple cake mix
1 can (20 oz.) crushed pineapple
1/2 cup vegetable oil
3 eggs
1/3 cup melted butter
2/3 cup packed brown sugar
maraschino cherries
cooking spray
cupcake/muffin baking tins (enough to make two dozen cupcakes)
electric mixer
mixing bowls, large and small
knife
cookie sheet

1. Spray cooking spray into the cups of the baking tins.
2. Preheat your oven to 350°F.
3. Slice 12 of the cherries in half; set aside.
4. Drain the pineapple, setting aside the juice.
5. Using electric mixer, beat cake mix, oil, eggs, and pineapple juice in a large bowl, first at low speed for 30 seconds, then at medium speed for 2 minutes.
6. In a different, smaller bowl, mix brown sugar and melted butter.
7. Spoon 1-1/2 teaspoons of the sugar-butter blend into each cup of the baking tins.
8. Spoon some pineapple and a cherry half into each cup.
9. Pour cake batter into each cup until about three-fourths full.
10. Bake 20–25 minutes or until a toothpick stuck into the center comes out clean.

11. After letting the cupcakes cool, use a knife to loosen them around the edges and turn them upside down onto cookie sheet.

Yield: 24 cupcakes

(Adapted from http://www.bettycrocker.com/recipes/pineapple-upside -down-cupcakes/c30fa990-ecf3-4664-a8e1-0a50c8c5c0a8 and http://www .tasteofhome.com/recipes/mini-pineapple-upside-down-cakes.)

Youth Study Book

INTRODUCTION:
THE STORY THROUGH MARY'S EYES

How Did She Feel?

One of my favorite Christmas albums is an old one released by the British singer-songwriter Roger Whittaker in 1978. My favorite track is a song called "Momma Mary." In it, the singer goes through the biblical Christmas story, and at several points—the angel Gabriel's visit to Mary in verse one, the arrival in Bethlehem in verse two, the coming of the shepherds and wise men in verse three—he asks Mary, "How did you feel? How did you feel?"

I'm not claiming "Momma Mary" is the world's best Christmas song. It wouldn't burn up any charts today. (I don't think it did back in 1978, either.) But I like it because it appeals to my love of stories. If I were writing a version of the Christmas story, one of my main interests would be how Mary felt and what Mary thought about all that was going on. That's because, like you, I'm used to modern storytelling. I like TV shows, movies, and novels that feature well-developed, psychologically interesting characters.

Biblical authors didn't share that priority. Their priority was proclaiming God's mighty acts for God's people and for the world. They focused on communicating God's urgent messages, not on crafting great literature.

Is there great literature in the Bible? Without a doubt! It didn't become the most influential book in Western civilization just because the church said it was important. And there are plenty of interesting human characters in Scripture, too. But their characterization is often subtle, just under the surface. Often you have to tease it out by reading between the lines, or by unpacking the nuances of the Greek or Hebrew words that the authors chose to use. Since characterization, as we're used to it, isn't front and center, we sometimes forget that the people in the Bible weren't two-dimensional cardboard cutouts or even fancy, but flat figures, in stained glass.

So when I first heard "Momma Mary," I heard an invitation to treat the Christmas story as a story, and its characters as characters. What *would* it feel like to learn that you had been chosen to be the mother of God's son? Or to find no room in Bethlehem after a long and exhausting journey? Or to have strangers ranging from humble shepherds to exotic sages bowing down before your baby? How *would* all that feel?

Contemplating Christmas with Mary

As it turns out, "Momma Mary" is one biblical person whose feelings and thoughts we occasionally do get to glimpse directly, especially in Luke's Gospel. She is, at various points, "confused" (1:29), "joyful" (1:47), "amazed" (2:18, 33), and "worried" (2:48).

But above all, Mary is contemplative. "Mary committed these things to memory," Luke tells us toward the end of his Christmas story, "and considered them carefully" (2:19). A bit later, we read that Mary "cherished every word" her young son spoke "in her heart" (2:51). Mary is doing more than simply being thoughtful. New Testament scholar Beverly Roberts Gaventa writes, "Mary is one who *reflects* on events.... Mary does not wait passively for someone else to explain things to her; she takes an active part by thinking, reflecting, considering matters." Dr. Gaventa explains that Mary "is not writing in the family scrapbook," but is, in effect, acting as the first Christian theologian.[1]

In modern American culture, the month leading up to Christmas isn't generally treated as time for thoughtful contemplation! Holiday decorating, shopping, and partying all occupy people's attention. Bright, blinking lights and loud, holly-jolly songs fill up the silences we could be using to ponder the season's significance. Our culture has decided that December is not a month for deep thought.

On the Christian calendar, in contrast, the four weeks before Christmas are set aside for contemplation. In the season of Advent, the church gives us the opportunity to reflect on Jesus' coming (the Latin word *adventus* means "coming"): his coming two thousand years ago as a baby, his promised coming in the future as ruler of God's new creation, and his coming through the Holy Spirit into our lives today. Until we think about all three dimensions of Jesus' coming, we can't begin to grasp all that he means for us and for our world.

Even as we take part in the fun and festivities of our culture's Christmas celebrations, it's important to take some time to follow Mary's lead and commit God's deeds to memory, consider them carefully, and cherish the words of Jesus in our hearts.

About This Book

This book is designed to help you create your own contemplative experience during Advent. It is based on and intended to complement Adam Hamilton's book *Not a Silent Night: Mary Looks Back to Bethlehem* (Abingdon Press, 2014). It follows the same structure: it looks backward at Jesus' life through Mary's eyes, beginning with his ascension and ending with his nativity. It uses the same chapter headings and key Scripture passages that *Not a Silent Night* uses, and touches on some of the same themes; however, you do not need to read *Not a Silent Night* in order to use and benefit from this book.

While you can use this book on your own, it can also be the basis for a group study, perhaps even one that your youth ministry or Sunday school takes on as part of a congregationwide Advent study. Each of the first four chapters includes the following elements of a session plan:

- **Lighting the Advent Candles**—A brief ritual of candle-lighting and responsive reading to help focus on God and to establish a contemplative tone

- **Scripture Focus**—The central Bible text to contemplate, printed without chapter and verse numbers (which were added to Scripture centuries later) to help you deal directly with the text
- **Mary Ponders**—A monologue from Mary's perspective, using some creative license to help us imagine what Jesus' mother felt and thought at key points of her son's life
- **Reading for Reflection**—A devotional essay that can help you begin reflecting on how the session's focal Scripture intersects with your life and faith
- **Meditating with Art**—A work of art interpreting the session's focal Scripture, offered, with brief background information, as a tool for your own prayer and meditation
- **Meditating with Music**—Options of music you can seek out and listen to (all the options are easily and legally available online) as part of your prayer and reflection
- *Lectio Divina*—Another Scripture passage, thematically related to the focal Scripture, which you are encouraged to read slowly and contemplatively several times, listening for how God may be speaking to you through its words
- **Ponder Giving This Present**—Suggestions and opportunities for gift-giving that has the potential to help change people's lives, as an alternative to the excessively materialistic spending that usually dominates cultural Christmas
- **This Week, Wonder With God About . . .**—A selection of daily Bible readings that expand on the themes and issues raised in each session, for your use in personal or family devotions

The additional helps in the Youth Leader Guide for this study include extra questions for study and discussion, as well as instructions for craft projects and recipes related to the topics and themes of each of the four main sessions.

While this resource does not include a complete session for Christmas Eve or Christmas Day, it does offer (in the fifth chapter) a candle-lighting ritual you can use as part of your personal or family devotions, as well as a final monologue from Mary and a new set of lyrics for "Silent Night" that reflect the same reality Adam Hamilton's book highlights: very little about that first Christmas, or about Mary's life as Jesus' mother, was silent!

Mary, Our Sister

As we'll soon see, different Christians view Mary in different ways. Some think of her as important only because she was Jesus' mother. Others hold a very high view of her, calling her "Queen of Heaven" and regarding her, in some sense, as their spiritual mother.

However else we may view Mary, she was—and still is, because to God all are alive (Luke 20:38)—our sister in the faith. She was among her son's first followers when they received the Holy Spirit and started their mission of spreading the good news. She saw and took part in the earliest spread of "the Way," as the Christian church was first known. For this reason alone, Mary deserves our attention and respect. She is a member of that "great cloud of witnesses surrounding us" (Hebrews 12:1), encouraging us to continue faithfully following her son.

May the time you spend with Mary this Advent, contemplating the life of her son and what he means for your life, lead you to sing along with her, "With all my heart I glorify the Lord! In the depths of who I am I rejoice in God my savior" (Luke 1:46-47).

1.

BEGINNING WITH THE END

Lighting the Advent Candles

The Lord be with you!
And also with you!

Keep the Lord before you always, for with God at your right hand, you shall
not be moved.
My heart is glad; my soul rejoices; my body, too, rests unafraid.
O God, you will not abandon us to the grave, or let your faithful followers
see the pit, but will show us the path of life.
**In your presence is fullness of joy, and in your right hand are pleasures
forevermore.**

—Based on Psalm 16:8-11

Scripture Focus
Acts 1:1-14

Theophilus, the first scroll I wrote concerned everything Jesus did and taught from the beginning, right up to the day when he was taken up into heaven. Before he was taken up, working in the power of the Holy Spirit, Jesus instructed the apostles he had chosen. After his suffering, he showed them that he was alive with many convincing proofs. He appeared to them over a period of forty days, speaking to them about God's kingdom. While they were eating together, he ordered them not to leave Jerusalem but to wait for what the Father had promised. He said, "This is what you heard from me: John baptized with water, but in only a few days you will be baptized with the Holy Spirit."

As a result, those who had gathered together asked Jesus, "Lord, are you going to restore the kingdom to Israel now?"

Jesus replied, "It isn't for you to know the times or seasons that the Father has set by his own authority. Rather, you will receive power when the Holy Spirit has come upon you, and you will be my witnesses in Jerusalem, in all Judea and Samaria, and to the end of the earth."

After Jesus said these things, as they were watching, he was lifted up and a cloud took him out of their sight. While he was going away and as they were staring toward heaven, suddenly two men in white robes stood next to them. They said, "Galileans, why are you standing here, looking toward heaven? This Jesus, who was taken up from you into heaven, will come in the same way that you saw him go into heaven."

Then they returned to Jerusalem from the Mount of Olives, which is near Jerusalem—a sabbath day's journey away. When they entered the city, they went to the upstairs room where they were staying. Peter, John, James, and Andrew; Philip and Thomas; Bartholomew and Matthew; James, Alphaeus' son; Simon the zealot; and Judas, James' son—all were united in their devotion to prayer, along with some women, including Mary the mother of Jesus, and his brothers.

Mary Ponders

They don't understand why I'm laughing. I don't blame them. To hear Peter tell it, what they've just seen on the Mount of Olives was amazing, not amusing! So the disciples aren't sure what I find so funny. Judging from the sidelong glances James and John are trading with each other, they may even worry that I've gone mad.

They're too polite to say so. They've never shown me anything but respect. I've told them, as I've always told everyone, I'm just another person. But I appreciate why they treat me as they do. For years, no one was closer to him than I was, and no one knew him better. But now I'm one of them, one of their many sisters. Yes, I tell them stories about what he was like as a child—they love hearing about that Passover when he was twelve; and they ask about the night of his birth, of course, wondering how holy and peaceful it must have been (I haven't yet had the heart to break it to them…)—but being his mother doesn't earn me any blessing that isn't available to them, too. (He made that clear while teaching a crowd in Nazareth once—I'll never forget that!)

So why am I laughing? Because Peter's report made me think: After all these years, I'm still waiting for my son!

The nine months I spent waiting for him the first time seemed to last forever. Sometimes I'd rub my swelling belly and ask him to hurry up. His conception had been a miracle; why couldn't the pregnancy be miraculous, too? It wasn't. I went through all the aches and pains, the wondering and worrying, that all expectant mothers know. But when he finally arrived, I knew only the joy of beholding him face to face, at last, and all my waiting faded away.

This time I won't be waiting long—"not many days from now," Peter said they were told—and I'm not waiting alone. This upper room is full of people my son touched and changed forever. We're family to each other, knit together not by blood but by the fact that he called us together to be his witnesses. He chose us to tell and to show what God is doing.

And what God is doing is changing everything! When I watched Jesus die, I was certain God had abandoned not only him but the entire world. How could God be present in a world where the power of death could claim such a victim, one who'd done nothing but teach and heal and help and love?

But then God raised him! I saw my son alive again. He was changed, but he was still my son. I could touch him, I could eat with him, I could talk with him. I could see in his new life a promise of new life for all. God is refusing to let death rule this world.

Now, he is gone again—but he lives. And I'm waiting to see him again. I know I will. I know he will be with us when the power he has promised us comes. He will go on teaching and healing and helping and loving—through us. We will see him reflected in each other.

And I will see him again when I die. Because though death will someday take me, it will not own me. I belong, as my new family does, to my son, who died but lives forever. And we will all know only the joy of beholding him face to face, at last, and all our waiting will fade away.

I know from experience what joy that is. And so, as we devote ourselves to prayer and we wait, I laugh. As the psalmist sang, my mouth is filled with laughter, and my tongue with shouts of joy, for God has done great things—for me, for us, for the world. Jesus—my son, God's son, the Savior—is alive!

Reading for Reflection

Mary for Many Seasons

Pop quiz! At what time of year are you most likely to think about these people?

- The Pilgrims
- George Washington and Abraham Lincoln
- Mary, the mother of Jesus

Unless you happen to live in Massachusetts, you probably think of the Pilgrims at Thanksgiving.

You most likely think of Washington and Lincoln together when Presidents' Day (and, if you're lucky, a day off from school) rolls around each February. (You also get credit if you answered, "Independence Day.")

But is Mary someone to think about only during the Advent and Christmas seasons?

No question, she makes a strong showing in December. She's in Nativity scenes on people's lawns, and hanging in ornament form on Christmas trees. She's gracing many greeting cards and is annually featured on a set of postage stamps. Hardly any Christmas pageant is complete without a girl or young woman in a blue bedsheet bringing Mary to life.

Most Protestant Christians only pay attention to Mary at this time of year. But in other branches of the Christian family, especially Roman Catholicism and Eastern Orthodoxy, Mary is a familiar face all year long. Her special days on these Christians' calendars include March 25, the Feast of the Annunciation, when the angel Gabriel told her she would be Jesus' mother (nine months before Christmas); May 31, the Feast of the Visitation (Mary's visit to Elizabeth); and September 8, the traditional date of Mary's own birth.

In the Bible, Mary features most prominently in Matthew and Luke's "Christmas stories." As this session's story from Acts proves, however, she shows up later as well. She saw Jesus' whole life and ministry: his birth in Bethlehem, his teaching and healing work in Nazareth and elsewhere, his crucifixion on Calvary—and, ultimately, his resurrection and ascension. She had a special perspective on Jesus. Whether or not your church observes her several feast days, she certainly merits more than once-a-year attention, not so much because of who she is but because of what she can show us about following her son.

The Crown of Life

In some Roman Catholic parishes, the entire month of May is devoted to Mary. Church members attend special services to crown statues or pictures of Mary with beautiful spring flowers. They do this to show respect and affection for the woman who bore and raised Jesus Christ. These "coronations" of

Mary mirror the belief that, after she died and entered eternal life, she became "Queen of Heaven."

The Bible never gives Mary that title. But it *does* tell us—indirectly—that, in her new life, she was crowned.

The apostle Paul wrote to his protégé, the young pastor Timothy, that the risen Lord will give "the champion's wreath"—the crown of laurels awarded in ancient Greece and Rome to runners who won races—"to all those who have set their heart on waiting for his appearance" (2 Timothy 4:8). Paul liked using the image of the victor's wreath to capture the success and joy awaiting people who persevere in faith. He wrote to early Christians in Corinth, for example, that athletes race "to get a crown of leaves that shrivel up and die, but we do it to receive a crown that never dies" (1 Corinthians 9:25). The crown Christ will give his followers is "the crown of life" (James 1:12, NRSV)—new, eternal life. And although Paul, James, and other writers in Scripture compare it to a prize, this crown is not a reward we can win. It's a gift we can only accept, once we have finished whatever course God sets before us.

As we will discover this Advent, the course God set for Mary was no quick sprint. It was a lifelong marathon! From the time she answered God's call, as a teenager, to be Jesus' mother, to the last time we see her in Scripture, in today's story, waiting with the rest of Jesus' disciples for the coming of the Holy Spirit, Mary spent her life racing to remain faithful to God. It can't have always been easy. Surely, like all of us, she stumbled along the way. (For example, check out the way she and his siblings tried to rein in Jesus in Mark 3:20-21, 31-35—we'll come back to that story later.) But she finished as a believer in her son and as a member of his community of witnesses, waiting for his appearance and for the fulfillment of God's good plan for the world.

Waiting with Mary

Mary's cameo in Acts marks her last appearance in the Bible. With the rest of Jesus' first followers, she is waiting for the coming of the Holy Spirit, the divine power that will energize her and the rest of her brothers and sisters to be Jesus' witnesses, in word and deed, in Jerusalem and far beyond (Acts 1:8). But did Mary's waiting take the form of "just waiting around"? Not likely!

How do we know? I think we have a clue in John's Gospel. For whatever reason, John never mentions Mary's name. He only calls her Jesus' mother, maybe to make certain his readers' attention remains on Jesus, where it belongs. If that was John's motive, I think Mary would have approved. After all, she was the one who told servants at a wedding party in Cana about her son, "Do whatever he tells you" (John 2:5).

I don't know what you'd tell *your* mother, father, or guardian to do if you expected they would obey whatever you told them! But Jesus told his mother, along with the rest of his followers, to love each other as he loved them (John 13:34)…to feed hungry people, clothe naked people, visit lonely people, and care for sick people (Matthew 25:34-40)…to seek God's rule and God's righteousness in all they did (Matthew 6:33)…to love God with their whole being, and to love their neighbors as themselves (Mark 12:29-31).

In Advent, we wait. We wait to celebrate Jesus' birth once more. We wait for his promised return in the future, when he will fully and finally rule over God's new heaven and new earth. We wait for him to come into our hearts every day, at any moment, through his Holy Spirit. But Jesus has given us plenty to do while we wait! He doesn't expect our waiting to take the form of "just waiting around," any more than Mary's did.

So this Advent, let's wait as Mary waited. Let's do whatever Jesus tells us to do, and go wherever he shows us to go, and love whomever he asks us to love. And as we do, let's remember that we do so in grateful anticipation of wearing the same crown Mary wears, the same crown all who have waited for Jesus wear: the crown of new and everlasting life.

Meditating with Art

The mosaic shown on the following page is located in the Neamţ Monastery in Romania. Although this monastic community was founded in the fourteenth century, the present building dates from 1497; it is named for the "Ascension of the Lord."[1]

"Ascension of the Lord," Neamț Monastery, Romania
(For a full-color image, visit Shutterstock.com and search for 35238970)

This scene shows Jesus ascending to heaven from the Mount of Olives (you can see the footprints he left behind) against a bright, gold-leaf background. In the foreground, we see Mary, Jesus' mother, among the disciples. Unlike the men, Mary is looking neither skyward toward her departing son nor at the two angels (the white-robed men of Acts 1:10, indicated as angels here by their haloes). Mary's focus remains steadfastly elsewhere.

Meditating with Music

Option A. "I Want to Walk as a Child of the Light" (words and music, Kathleen Thomerson, 1966).

- Which words, phrases, or images from this song most grab your attention, and why?
- How does this song express confident Christian hope?

Option B. Regina Coeli ("Queen of Heaven") is an ancient Latin hymn from the Roman Catholic tradition, sung especially during the Easter season. One English translation of the Latin text reads:

> Queen of heaven, rejoice, alleluia:
> For He whom you merited to bear, alleluia,
> Has risen, as He said, alleluia.
> Pray for us to God, alleluia.[2]

Some Protestant Christians may feel uncomfortable calling Mary "Queen of Heaven" or asking her to pray for them. All Christians, however, can appreciate this hymn's emphasis on the joy of Jesus' resurrection, as well as the hymn's repeated summons to praise God—which is what the word *alleluia* literally means.

Locate and listen to a setting of *Regina Coeli*.

- How does the music capture the text's spirit of joy?
- How does praising God for Jesus' resurrection increase our joyful anticipation of our own resurrection to come?

Lectio Divina
2 Timothy 4:1-8

I'm giving you this commission in the presence of God and of Christ Jesus, who is coming to judge the living and the dead, and by his appearance and his kingdom. Preach the word. Be ready to do it whether it is convenient or inconvenient. Correct, confront, and encourage with patience and instruction. There will come a time when people will not tolerate sound teaching. They will collect teachers who say what they want to hear because they are self-centered. They will turn their back on the truth and turn to myths. But you must keep control of yourself in all circumstances. Endure suffering, do the work of a preacher of the good news, and carry out your service fully.

I'm already being poured out like a sacrifice to God, and the time of my death is near. I have fought the good fight, finished the race, and kept the faith. At last the champion's wreath that is awarded for righteousness is waiting for me. The Lord, who is the righteous judge, is going to give it to me on that day. He's giving it not only to me but also to all those who have set their heart on waiting for his appearance.

Ponder Giving This Present: Spread the Word

Just before his Ascension, Jesus promised his followers that they would serve him as witnesses "to the end of the earth" (Acts 1:8). You may not be able to travel so far abroad, but you can help ensure that the Scriptures do.

The American Bible Society (ABS) provides people around the world, as well as in the United States, access to the Bible where before they had none. Since its founding in 1816, the ABS has been translating and providing Bibles for populations who haven't before had access to the Scriptures in their own language. And the ABS today does more than simply distribute Bibles (although there's nothing "simple" about its vast distribution programs). According to its website, the ABS brings together biblical and mental health resources "to equip local churches to care for people with deep emotional and spiritual injuries caused by war, domestic violence, natural disasters and other traumatic events," including sexual violence. It also reaches out to youth worldwide who have been abandoned or harmed by domestic or gang violence, to "restore broken spirits with Scripture"; and offers customized Bible programs for members of the U.S. Armed Forces and their families.[3]

To learn more about the ABS and about how your donations can help its work, browse the ABS gift catalog at http://gift.americanbible.org/. You may also want to find out what Bible translation or distribution ministries your denomination or congregation already supports, and plan ways to encourage others to join you in supporting those efforts.

This Week, Wonder with God About...

Sunday – Psalm 33

What reasons does the psalm-singer give for praising God? What connection does the psalm-singer make between waiting for God and experiencing joy?

Monday – John 17:1-3

We tend to think of "eternal life" as life with God in heaven, but, according to these verses, how does eternal life begin here and now?

Tuesday – 2 Peter 3:8-13

How does Peter answer those who say that God is taking too much time to keep God's promises about the future? What are Christians waiting for, and how does Peter instruct them to wait for it?

Wednesday – John 10:27-30

Jesus, our Good Shepherd, promises that nothing can snatch us out of his hand. How does this promise encourage you to remain faithful to him? How are you listening for Jesus' voice today?

Thursday – John 11:17-27

"Do you believe this?" (verse 26). When do you find it easy to believe that Jesus is the resurrection and the life? When do you find it more difficult? Whom can you help believe the good news, and how?

Friday – Revelation 12:1-12

This part of John's vision is a richly symbolic affirmation that God's power will prevail over all evil. (Some Christians identify Mary as the woman with the starry crown who gives birth to the male child.) How do you find courage when you face evil in your life or witness it at work in the world?

Saturday – 1 Corinthians 15:17-28

These verses are part of Paul's impassioned argument about why Jesus' resurrection matters. What's at stake, according to the apostle? How are your actions today influenced by the promise that God will one day bring everything, even death, under Christ's control?

2.

THE PIERCING OF MARY'S SOUL

Lighting the Advent Candles

The Lord be with you!
And also with you!

Like a young plant he grew up before us, like a root from dry ground.
He was not beautiful to behold; nothing about his appearance drew us to him.
We despised him, and hid our faces from him; we thought God struck him down and afflicted him.
But he was wounded for our transgressions, and crushed for our sins, and he bore the punishment that made us whole.

—Based on Isaiah 53:2-5

Scripture Focus
Luke 2:21-35 (NIV)

On the eighth day, when it was time to circumcise the child, he was named Jesus, the name the angel had given him before he was conceived.

When the time came for the purification rites required by the Law of Moses, Joseph and Mary took him to Jerusalem to present him to the Lord (as it is written in the Law of the Lord, "Every firstborn male is to be consecrated to the Lord"), and to offer a sacrifice in keeping with what is said in the Law of the Lord: "a pair of doves or two young pigeons."

Now there was a man in Jerusalem called Simeon, who was righteous and devout. He was waiting for the consolation of Israel, and the Holy Spirit was on him. It had been revealed to him by the Holy Spirit that he would not die before he had seen the Lord's Messiah. Moved by the Spirit, he went into the temple courts. When the parents brought in the child Jesus to do for him what the custom of the Law required, Simeon took him in his arms and praised God, saying:

"Sovereign Lord, as you have promised,
   you may now dismiss your servant in peace.
For my eyes have seen your salvation,
   which you have prepared in the sight of all nations:
a light for revelation to the Gentiles,
   and the glory of your people Israel."

The child's father and mother marveled at what was said about him. Then Simeon blessed them and said to Mary, his mother: "This child is destined to cause the falling and rising of many in Israel, and to be a sign that will be spoken against, so that the thoughts of many hearts will be revealed. And a sword will pierce your own soul too."

Mary Ponders

There are some things you *don't* say to a new mother. I've only been one for six weeks, but I know this is true.

You don't tell her she looks tired. *You* try getting up at all hours to feed, change, and cuddle a baby. See how well-rested *you* look!

You don't tell her she's holding her baby wrong. I haven't dropped Jesus on his head once, have I? Besides, he's one of those babies who likes to look out. He doesn't *want* to be held close all the time. He wants and needs to face the world.

And you *definitely* don't tell a new mother her baby is destined for trouble.

What arrogance! God may well write all our days in his scroll before we are born, as King David sang in the psalms. But David's son Solomon wrote that no one can read what God will do from our beginning to our end.

And even if you somehow knew God had written days of trouble for a baby... for *my* baby... what would possibly possess you to say so?

Simeon. What a *strange* man. He ran up to Joseph and me at the Temple so quickly, he almost knocked us over. He took Jesus in his arms—without asking! I've gotten used to people wanting to hold the baby (if only to show me how I'm doing it wrong), but they always ask permission!

Not Simeon. He just scooped Jesus up! I was shocked. I couldn't find my voice to shout, "Give me back my baby!" I slapped Joseph on the arm, trying to get him to do something.

Then Simeon started chanting. I listened, amazed. He was thanking God for showing him the light of salvation.

There's no way this stranger could have known we'd given the baby a name that means "God saves," as the angel told us to. But here he was, warbling in his raspy voice that our baby would show God's glory—to Israel, and to Gentiles, too.

When he finished singing, he handed Jesus back with a huge smile. Somehow, I managed to smile back a little bit. Jesus was safe in my arms again, after all, and Simeon was now giving our family a blessing.

But *then*! Then he ruined it all by telling me my child would cause conflict and division in Israel.

Hadn't he just finished praising God for sending my baby to be a Savior?

I was so confused, so furious. I wanted to tell Simeon he was wrong. I wanted to tell him what the angel told us about Jesus being king. I wanted to tell him what the shepherds in Bethlehem had said—they called the baby "Lord"!

But before I could say anything, Simeon said, with wild, wide eyes, "And a sword will pierce your soul." And then he left, as quickly as he'd come.

He might as well have punched me in the stomach. I gasped for breath. My whole body shook as I started to cry. Joseph tried to hug me, but I pulled away. I just wanted to hug my baby. I just wanted to hold on to Jesus, to smother him with kisses, to pull him so close that no stranger in this strange world could ever snatch him away again.

He struggled against me, waving his little arms, kicking his little legs.

Because he likes to look out. Because he wants and needs to face the world.

Reading for Reflection

Mary at the Cross

The Gospels don't let us forget this truth. In Matthew's Gospel, King Herod is the "monster at the manger," sending soldiers to slay baby boys in and around Bethlehem for fear one of them will take his place as king of the Jews (Matthew 2:16-18). And in Luke's Gospel, the prophet Simeon, led by the Holy Spirit to find Mary, Joseph, and the baby at the Temple in Jerusalem, includes this dark message for Mary in his otherwise joyous song: "This child is destined to be a sign that will be rejected; and you too will be pierced to the heart" (Luke 2:34-35, Revised English Bible).

Simeon's words probably hurt to hear, but I'm sure Mary pondered them now and then as Jesus grew up. Once Jesus started teaching and healing, she might have thought Simeon was preparing her for the pain she'd feel as her son left to face the world. He attracted disciples, but also "generate[d] opposition," as Simeon had predicted (2:34)—including powerful opposition from religious authorities.

Good mothers never stop worrying about their kids. Mary probably worried about her son's reputation—honor and shame were constant concerns in that society—and may even have feared for his life. We can understand why she and his siblings tried "to take control of him" one time (Mark 3:21)—and we can imagine how Jesus' answer might have stung the woman who gave him birth: "Who is my mother? Who are my brothers?...Whoever does God's will is my brother, sister, and mother" (3:33, 35).

Whatever pain Mary felt watching Jesus embrace followers as family, it cannot have matched the stabbing grief she felt watching him die. John says nothing about Mary's state of mind as she stands near the cross (John 19:25); he doesn't have to. Crucifixion was the Roman Empire's cruelest form of capital punishment. It was so sadistic in the way it maximized suffering that it gave Latin, and later English, a new word to describe intense pain: *excruciating.*

Watching a complete stranger's crucifixion would be hard enough. Watching a family member die is hard enough. How terrible must it have been for Mary to watch her son die like this? Whether Mary thought about Simeon's prophecy or not, she felt the piercing he had told her would come.

Dealing with Sin

Not even Mary knew the full meaning of Jesus' death until after his resurrection. Why had he died? Why in this way? Years later, the Apostle Paul tried to explain: "God caused the one who didn't know sin to be sin for our sake..." (2 Corinthians 5:21).

More than the individual sins we commit, sin is a force fundamentally opposed to God's good will. It doesn't belong in the world, but it's here, dangerous and wild. In Genesis, God warned Cain that sin is like a beast "waiting at the door ready to strike!" (Genesis 4:7). God urged Cain to master it. Instead, Cain killed his brother.

We *can't* master sin. Only God can. So God entered our world in Jesus, taking the fight against sin to sin's own falsely claimed turf—being born as one of us, in the shadow cast by sin, at risk from evil and death because of it, as we all are. In Jesus' death, God judges the power of sin. When we see the cross, we see sin exposed as the ugly monstrosity it is.

But we also see the depth of God's love. Paul went on to say that Jesus died as he did "so that through him we could become the righteousness of God" (2 Corinthians 5:21). In Jesus, God suffered the condemnation that we, as sin's servants—sometimes unwillingly, sometimes more than willingly—

deserve. God utterly "destroyed the record of the debt we owed...by nailing it to the cross" (Colossians 2:14). As an angel had told Joseph before Jesus' birth, Jesus—Emmanuel, God With Us—"save[s] his people from their sins" (Matthew 1:21, 23), and from sin itself.

Here Is Your Family

Even though God, in Jesus, saves us from sin, we still feel sin's effects, still struggle against temptation, and still see evil and death destroying human lives and the world. Sin is doomed but continues to cast a big, ugly shadow. We need that new family Jesus spoke about, those new brothers and sisters and fathers and mothers who obey God.

From his cross, Jesus faced a world still in sin's shadow. He also saw "his mother and the disciple whom he loved" (John 19:26). Bible scholars debate who that disciple was; I wonder how much it matters, because Jesus loved—and loves—*all* his disciples. What we know is that Jesus entrusted Mary and this disciple to each other: "Woman, here is your son.... Here is your mother" (19:26-27).

Jesus gave us each other to face God's much-loved but sin-shadowed world together. He brings us together to love each other as he loved us, and to encourage one another to do all the good God has given us to do. He sends us into the world to be his witnesses, and to look on and love everyone as our family—all of us sinners, whom God calls, again and again, to the foot of the cross to see God's amazing grace.

Meditating with Art

The artistic depiction, usually in sculpture, of Mary holding and grieving her dead son is called a *pieta*. The word is Italian and derives from the Latin word for "piety," or dutiful religious devotion. In pietas, Jesus' wounds are usually visible, and Mary usually appears youthful.

The Renaissance artist Michelangelo sculpted one of the world's most famous pietas, found at the Vatican. The pieta shown in this photograph is in the Church of Saint Alexander of Bergamo in Zebedia, located in Milan, Italy. According to tradition, the original church building on this site was built on

"Pieta," Church of Saint Alexander of Bergamo in Zebedia, Milan, Italy
(For a full-color image, visit Shutterstock.com and search for 86475064)

the ruins of the place where Alexander, a Roman soldier, was imprisoned and ultimately beheaded in A.D. 303 for refusing to give up his faith in Christ.

Meditating with Music

Option A. "Mary, Did You Know?" (words and music by Mark Lowry and Buddy Greene)

- What questions would you ask Mary about what it was like to be Jesus' mother?
- What questions do you have about how Jesus is the Savior?

Option B. "Mary Speaks" (lyrics by Madeleine L'Engle, music by Daniel Gawthrop)

- How would you describe the tone or mood of this song?
- What specific image(s) in this song most grab your attention? Why?
- How does this song influence the way you think about Mary, and about Jesus?

Lectio Divina
John 19:23-30

When the soldiers crucified Jesus, they took his clothes and his sandals, and divided them into four shares, one for each soldier. His shirt was seamless, woven as one piece from the top to the bottom. They said to each other, "Let's not tear it. Let's cast lots to see who will get it." This was to fulfill the Scripture,

They divided my clothes among themselves,
*   and they cast lots for my clothing.*

That's what the soldiers did.

Jesus' mother and his mother's sister, Mary the wife of Clopas, and Mary Magdalene stood near the cross. When Jesus saw his mother and the disciple whom he loved standing nearby, he said to his mother, "Woman, here is your son." Then he said to the disciple, "Here is your mother." And from that time on, this disciple took her into his home.

After this, knowing that everything was already completed, in order to fulfill the Scripture, Jesus said, "I am thirsty." A jar full of sour wine was nearby, so the soldiers soaked a sponge in it, placed it on a hyssop branch, and held it up to his lips. When he had received the sour wine, Jesus said, "It is completed." Bowing his head, he gave up his life.

Ponder Giving This Present:
Newborns in Need

Mary and Joseph sacrificed "a pair of turtledoves or two young pigeons" (Luke 2:24) because they were poor parents and could not afford sheep

(Leviticus 12:8). Helping infants born into poverty, then, is especially appropriate as we celebrate the birth of the Savior.

Newborns in Need (NIN) is a national charity, "founded upon Christian principles of love and acceptance," that provides items necessary for caring for "premature, ill, or impoverished newborns" free of charge. NIN welcomes donations of the following items (and more—see the complete list at http:// newbornsinneed.org/donate/our-wish-list/):

- Sleepers, gowns, undershirts, and onesies (preemie and newborn– three months)
- Clothing new and gently used from 3–6 months to 9–12 months
- Receiving blankets, quilts, fleece blankets, and afghans (30 by 30 and larger)
- Socks and booties
- Bibs, burp cloths, pacifiers, and bottles (BPA-free plastics)
- Toiletries and wipes, regular size and trial sizes
- Diapers and pull-ups (especially in newborn sizes)
- Baby formula

Items are accepted at NIN's local chapters (http://newbornsinneed. org/chapters/chapter-locator/), or a package can be sent to its national headquarters (5723 Country Club Road #R, Winston Salem, NC 27104). Perhaps your youth ministry can lead your congregation in collecting items such as these for NIN or a similar charity that helps the most vulnerable of babies receive the care they need.

This Week, Wonder with God About . . .

Sunday – Psalm 22

According to both Mark (15:34) and Matthew (27:46), Jesus echoed this psalm's words when he died. Read the whole psalm several times. How does the psalm-singer change from the psalm's beginning to its end? How does this change help you think about why Jesus might have quoted it from his cross?

Monday – Luke 23:39-43

In the Temple, Simeon predicted that Jesus would cause division. How do we see that division in these verses, even as Jesus is dying? Try making the second criminal's prayer your own: "Jesus, remember me when you come into your kingdom."

Tuesday – Luke 2:36-38

Simeon wasn't the only prophet who had something to say about Jesus that day in the Temple. How are you, like Anna, speaking about Jesus to others this holiday season?

Wednesday – Hebrews 2:10-17

God did not save us in Jesus resentfully or half-heartedly, but willingly and out of love. How do you react to hearing that Jesus "isn't ashamed to call [us] brothers and sisters" (v. 11)? How should Jesus' acceptance of us shape our attitude toward others?

Thursday – John 17:14-19

Before his arrest and execution, Jesus prayed not that God would take Jesus' followers out of the world but that God would keep them holy in the world. What does being holy while in this world look like? How are you tempted to forget that you belong not to this world but to God?

Friday – Romans 15:5-7

The Apostle Paul urges Christians to welcome each other so that they can become a community united in praise of God. How do you make newcomers to your youth ministry and congregation feel welcome? How does the welcome you give mirror the welcome into God's presence that Jesus gives us?

Saturday – Romans 8:35-39

Paul's jubilant trust in God's love in Christ is worth reading several times, and even memorizing. When have you wondered or feared that something might separate you from God's love? What would you say to, or do for, someone who is facing those same worries and fears?

3.

AMAZED, ASTOUNDED, AND ASTONISHED

Lighting the Advent Candles

The Lord be with you!
And also with you!

How lovely is your dwelling place, O LORD of hosts!
My soul longs, even yearns, for the courts of the LORD. My heart and body sing for joy to the living God!
Blessed are the ones who live in your home, forever singing your praise. I would rather be a doorkeeper in the house of my God than live comfortably in the tents of the wicked.
God is sun and shield, favor and glory. O LORD of hosts, blessed is everyone who trusts in you!

—Based on Psalm 84:1-2, 4, 10-12

Scripture Focus
Luke 2:40-52

The child grew up and became strong. He was filled with wisdom, and God's favor was on him.

Each year his parents went to Jerusalem for the Passover Festival. When he was 12 years old, they went up to Jerusalem according to their custom. After the festival was over, they were returning home, but the boy Jesus stayed behind in Jerusalem. His parents didn't know it. Supposing that he was among their band of travelers, they journeyed on for a full day while looking for him among their family and friends. When they didn't find Jesus, they returned to Jerusalem to look for him. After three days they found him in the temple. He was sitting among the teachers, listening to them and putting questions to them. Everyone who heard him was amazed by his understanding and his answers. When his parents saw him, they were shocked.

His mother said, "Child, why have you treated us like this? Listen! Your father and I have been worried. We've been looking for you!"

Jesus replied, "Why were you looking for me? Didn't you know that it was necessary for me to be in my Father's house?" But they didn't understand what he said to them.

Jesus went down to Nazareth with them and was obedient to them. His mother cherished every word in her heart. Jesus matured in wisdom and years, and in favor with God and with people.

Mary Ponders

Who *is* this boy?

I look at him stretched out on the floor of our tent, asleep after a long day's travel. He's getting so big. How could this tall, awkward twelve-year-old, still not comfortable in his own skin, ever have been inside my belly?

Amazing. I was only a little bit older than he is now when the angel came to tell me I would be his mother.

Who is he? And who will he be?

Do all mothers have these moments, when they feel like their children are strangers? It's humbling to think the little baby I once wrapped in swaddling clothes is fast becoming his own person, a unique individual with his own thoughts and feelings and dreams.

I remember the times I thought my parents didn't understand that about me. Sometimes I'm sure Jesus feels the same way. "Mother, stop," he'll say, when I fuss over how he's dressed before he leaves the house, or tousle his hair for too long. When he has children someday, he may realize that I really am trying to give him room to discover himself. I let him run wild with his friends, chasing a ball around our neighborhood in Nazareth. I haven't told him—yet—that I know he goes out of his way to walk past that one very pretty girl's house every afternoon. I let him stay up late more often than I should to help his father with the wood and stone—

His father . . .

I'm sure Joseph will never admit it, but I saw him flinch when Jesus said what he said in the Temple today. What is it about our son and the Temple? Twelve years ago, that strange old man Simeon, with his strange words . . . and today, in the same place, more strange words, this time from our own son's mouth.

And those after who knows how many hours' worth of strange words he'd been sharing with the rabbis. They were hanging on every one, those gray sages with their long beards, staring at Jesus as he recited Torah at length, and spoke so passionately about what it meant, and threw question after question at them, as though they were his students and not the other way around.

I could have hugged him and throttled him all at once. I grabbed him by the shoulders, demanding how he could have treated us like this, although I was even angrier at Joseph and myself for not having noticed he wasn't in our caravan. I was cursing myself for having been *too* lenient, *too* trusting. An especially frightening thought even flickered through my mind: "What will the Lord do to me, because I have lost this precious gift?"

31

I thought Jesus would say only, "Mother, stop." But his eyes were wide with innocence as he asked why we were worried, why we'd been looking for him. He was in his father's house—where else would he be?

Joseph said nothing as we took Jesus with us. I hadn't seen my husband's face so clouded by confusion since the day I told him the angel's message. I was and still am confused, too, of course.

And so I sit watching my son as he sleeps, no lines of worry troubling his face. I may not know exactly who he is. Maybe I never will. Maybe that's the way of being human. But *he* seems to know who he is, and who he will be.

And because I love him, how could I hope for more?

Reading for Reflection

The Dreaded Question

Maybe you like this question better than I did when I was a teenager. I would do all I could to avoid it: pretending I hadn't heard, burying my nose in a book, shrugging and changing the subject. The question made me uncomfortable, nervous, even sick to my stomach.

What was this intolerable interrogative?

"What do you want to do with your life?"

I had no idea. And I envied kids who did. One friend of mine wanted to be a Broadway star. Another wanted to be the next Steve Jobs or Bill Gates. Someone else was fired up to be an overseas missionary. I wondered, *How have they already figured this out?* I hadn't even figured out how to pass my driver's test, or how to ask the pretty girl at church to a movie. Yet plenty of my peers had mapped out their careers!

Once, I thought I'd found a good answer. I loved to read, I loved to write; I thought I might make a good high school English teacher. But when I told *my* high school English teacher this insight—thinking she'd be pleased, that she might even offer some advice to start me down the path—she sighed and said, "Oh, you can do better than *that*."

Ouch!

Teen Jesus

I wonder how Jesus, when he was a teenager, felt when grownups asked him what he wanted to do with his life.

Have you wondered what Jesus was like as a teen? The New Testament is silent on the subject. Today's story from Luke, in which Jesus is twelve years old, is the closest we come. Plenty of people, from ancient tall-tale spinners to modern novelists, have taken stabs at filling this gap in Jesus' biography. But authoritative info about Jesus' adolescence? We've got exactly *none*.

We *do* have Scripture's assurance that Jesus, while fully divine, was also fully human. The letter to the Hebrews tells us Jesus was like us in every respect, except he never sinned (2:14; 4:15)—which, if you think about sins as failures to be who God made us to be, means sinless Jesus was the *only* fully human being who's ever lived.

So while we don't know the specifics of Jesus' teen years, we can confidently conclude he thought and felt just about everything teens think and feel.

Were there days he wanted to sleep in and stay up late? I wouldn't be surprised.

Did the ups and downs of close friendships with other teens—intense heart-to-hearts, angry arguments, painful misunderstandings—sometimes leave him dizzied? Unquestionably.

Luke tells us Jesus obeyed his parents (2:51)—but did he also sometimes get frustrated with them? Sure. We may even hear a hint of impatience in his voice when he tells Mary she should have known where he'd be (2:49).

And I'm certain he sometimes dreaded that question, "What do you want to do with your life?" It's a big deal, discerning how your interests, experiences, talents, and skills can help you earn a living and make a difference. Trying to figure that out is bound to cause everyone at least a few stressful moments.

Being About God's Business

Born into poverty in Roman-occupied Palestine, Jesus had fewer options open to him than many teens have today. He couldn't simply follow his dreams wherever they might lead. (And, as much as we Americans like to tell ourselves otherwise, and as full of opportunity as our nation is, our birth, background, and social status shape *our* prospects more than we generally realize or admit.)

But I'd bet Jesus *did* have some dreams he wanted to pursue. Maybe he enjoyed working with wood and stone, like Joseph, and wanted to keep doing that work. Maybe he hoped to get married and raise a family. Maybe he planned to travel the Mediterranean world.

When we read about the boy Jesus in the Temple, we—like Mary, Joseph, and the teachers—are astonished at how different he was. People reacted to him that way a lot. And, no doubt: Jesus *was* different. He *was* special. Mary knew it; that's why she "cherished [his] every word in her heart" (Luke 2:51).

As astonishing as young Jesus was, however, don't forget: he was like us in every respect! While his relationship with God the Father is different than ours, we also are called to be in God's presence and to be focused on God's priorities. No matter where our lives take us, we're always supposed to stay in our Father's house.

Fun fact, no extra charge: The Greek text of verse 49 doesn't include the word house. In fact, there's no noun where one should be. Supplying the word makes sense, but in some older translations, Jesus says he must "be about [his] Father's business."

I've always liked that translation better. Yes, the Temple mattered to Jesus. Like the psalm-singer, he longed to be "in the LORD's courtyards" (Psalm 84:2), in that place above all places where ancient Jews expected to encounter God. But Jews then also believed—as devout Jews today believe, and as Christians believe—that God is everywhere. God is omnipresent (no charge for the fancy word, either). We can experience God's presence, hear God's word, and do God's work everywhere and anywhere.

It turns out that, for Christians, the question "What do you want to do with your life?" is no cause for dread. The letter to the Ephesians sums up our answer: "We are God's accomplishment, created in Christ Jesus to do good things. God planned these good things to be the way that we live our lives" (Ephesians 2:10).

God's Will for Our Lives

My friend who wanted to make it big on Broadway? He did. My friend who wanted to be a cutting-edge computer whiz? He teaches accounting, not computing. I have no idea if my would-be missionary friend followed that sense of call. And, to be honest, sometimes I'm *still* not sure I've figured out what to do with myself.

But I believe God can, does, and will use me wherever I am, whatever I'm doing. I believe God gives us all endless opportunities to be about God's business.

If you already know what you want to do with your life—great! Go for it! And if you aren't sure—don't panic! Finding and following God's will for your life isn't something we get one shot at, and if we mess up, too bad for us. Whatever specific path, or even paths, God intends us to walk, our general direction is clear: to love God and love our neighbor. God has already told us what is good: doing justice, loving mercy, and walking humbly with God (Micah 6:8).

Maybe Jesus knew, at twelve years old, exactly what God would call him to do. Maybe he didn't. But he knew God loved him and called him to live in that love and spread it to others, no matter what his future held.

May God help us know that same truth!

Meditating with Art

The illustration on the following page of today's Bible story depicts a variety of reactions to young Jesus; note the various facial expressions and postures of the teachers. The scene preserves the emotional content of Luke's account because it includes Mary and Joseph discovering their son. As in much Christian art, Joseph is shown as much older than Mary (notice his beard), even though the Bible never tells us Joseph's age. Because Joseph does not appear in the Bible after this story, readers have long assumed that he died before Jesus began his public ministry.

"Jesus Teaching in the Temple" (relief), Trnava, Slovakia
(For a full-color image, visit iStockPhoto.com and search for 36326602)

Meditating with Music

Option A. "O Sing a Song of Bethlehem" (words by Louis F. Benson, 1889)

- How does our celebration of Christmas suffer if we forget that the baby born in Bethlehem grew to become the man who died on Calvary, and who rose again?
- What, do you think, are "the flowers of Nazareth [that] in every heart may grow" (verse 2)? How are they growing in your heart?

Option B. "The Lord Is My Light" (Taizé community chant)

The Taizé community is an ecumenical monastic community, founded in France in 1940 by Brother Roger Schutz. According to the *New York Times*, Schutz "sought to create greater unity among Christian churches, but his focus above all was to awaken spirituality among the young people in Europe who were growing up in a secular world."[1] The Taizé community's distinctive, meditative musical chants have become a popular way of prayer around the world. Easily remembered once sung several times, they can be a way to enter the presence of God wherever you are, whatever you are doing.

Lectio Divina
Mark 12:28-34

One of the legal experts heard their dispute and saw how well Jesus answered them. He came over and asked him, "Which commandment is the most important of all?"

Jesus replied, "The most important one is *Israel, listen! Our God is the one Lord, and you must love the Lord your God with all your heart, with all your being, with all your mind, and with all your strength.* The second is this, *You will love your neighbor as yourself.* No other commandment is greater than these."

The legal expert said to him, "Well said, Teacher. You have truthfully said that God is one and there is no other besides him. And to love God with all of the heart, a full understanding, and all of one's strength, and to love one's neighbor as oneself is much more important than all kinds of entirely burned offerings and sacrifices."

When Jesus saw that he had answered with wisdom, he said to him, "You aren't far from God's kingdom." After that, no one dared to ask him any more questions.

Ponder Giving This Present:
School Supplies and Books

Jesus amazed the teachers in the Temple with his understanding of the Scriptures. His knowledge was much more than "book learning," of course; but the story can remind us of education's importance, especially for children who are growing up in poverty, as Jesus did. A good education can still provide students with information and opportunities that can help them make a better life for themselves.

Even though school supplies may be the last thing on your mind as Christmas is coming, there are probably kids in your community who could really use them. Start a collection of basic school supplies—as you likely know, many schools and school districts post required supply lists online—and donate them now or in the fall when a new academic year begins. Some congregations present new backpacks stuffed with school supplies to kids staying in homeless shelters; contact local shelter administrators to learn how you can help.

Also consider donating to programs that help impoverished students abroad. Books for Africa, for example, is "the largest shipper of donated text and library books to the African continent, shipping over 33 million books to 49 different countries since 1988" (www.booksforafrica.org/). Books for the Barrios distributes books to deprived regions in the Philippines (www.booksforthebarrios.org/). Both organizations, and others like them, accept donations of money and books.

This Week, Wonder with God About . . .

Sunday – Psalm 119:97-104

The psalm-singer claims to think about God's "Instruction," or Torah, "constantly" (v. 97), and even claims "greater insight than all [the] teachers" (v. 99). What subject, in or out of school, do you enjoy studying most? How does your passion for and persistence in that subject compare with your study of God's instruction in Scripture?

Monday – 1 Samuel 3:1-10

The story of twelve-year-old Jesus in the Temple may remind us of how young Samuel, who served the priest Eli, astounded him with a message from God. Unfortunately for Eli, the message God gave through Samuel was a message of judgment; but Eli accepted it as an authentic word from God. Samuel literally listened to God's voice. How do *you* tell God, "Your servant is listening"—and what do *you* hear, or expect to hear, in response?

Tuesday – Matthew 7:24-29

People continued to be amazed by Jesus' words when he grew up. What teaching from Jesus amazes you the most? Which of his words do you try to build your life on, as the wise person in his parable built a house upon a rock? Why do you think people recognized in Jesus an authority that they did not find in other teachers?

Wednesday – John 6:53-69

Sometimes people were not only amazed but also offended by what Jesus said. What teaching from Jesus surprises, confuses, or even shocks you? Why? When you have a hard time understanding what Jesus means, what do you do?

Thursday – Luke 3:21-22

Jesus' baptism confirmed the understanding he'd claimed as a boy about his special relationship with God. Christians believe that our baptism joins us to Jesus and that God calls us, too, beloved children in whom God finds great happiness. How do you remind yourself, on a daily basis, of your identity as a beloved child of God in Jesus? What difference does this identity make to you?

Friday – Romans 12:3-8

We sometimes think mostly about how we can use our gifts to find satisfaction and success for ourselves. While those goals are important, the Apostle Paul reminds us, in these verses, that one way we are to use God's gifts is for the good of the community of faith. How are you using your individual gifts to serve your Christian community? How are you using them to serve your neighbors outside the church?

Saturday – Colossians 3:17

Try memorizing this verse today. Finding God's will for our lives isn't always, or perhaps even usually, a matter of puzzling out "the one right thing" that God wants us to do. Instead, we find God's will when we do *everything* we're doing with gratitude to God and seeking God's glory. This week, how have you found God's will for you in this way?

4.

MARY, FULL OF GRACE

Lighting the Advent Candles

The Lord be with you!

And also with you!

From sunrise to sunset, let God's name be praised!

God is exalted above all nations;

God's glory is higher even than the heavens!

Who else is like the LORD our God, who rules from on high, but comes down to look on heaven and earth?

God lifts the poor from the dust and raises the needy from the rubbish to place them among the princes of God's people.

—Based on Psalm 113:3-8

Scripture Focus
Luke 1:26-38

When Elizabeth was six months pregnant, God sent the angel Gabriel to Nazareth, a city in Galilee, to a virgin who was engaged to a man named Joseph, a descendant of David's house. The virgin's name was Mary. When the angel came to her, he said, "Rejoice, favored one! The Lord is with you!" She was confused by these words and wondered what kind of greeting this might be. The angel said, "Don't be afraid, Mary. God is honoring you. Look! You will conceive and give birth to a son, and you will name him Jesus. He will be great and he will be called the Son of the Most High. The Lord God will give him the throne of David his father. He will rule over Jacob's house forever, and there will be no end to his kingdom."

Then Mary said to the angel, "How will this happen since I haven't had sexual relations with a man?"

The angel replied, "The Holy Spirit will come over you and the power of the Most High will overshadow you. Therefore, the one who is to be born will be holy. He will be called God's Son. Look, even in her old age, your relative Elizabeth has conceived a son. This woman who was labeled 'unable to conceive' is now six months pregnant. Nothing is impossible for God."

Then Mary said, "I am the Lord's servant. Let it be with me just as you have said." Then the angel left her.

Mary Ponders

I *should* be more scared than I am.

Sure, sometimes I'm scared. Sometimes I'm terrified! Here I am, a poor girl, not married and already pregnant. I'm not ready to be a mother. I'm barely ready to be a grownup!

I've worried what the neighbors will say when I get back home. In the three months I've been staying here with cousin Elizabeth and Zechariah, I've *definitely* started to show.

And I've imagined Joseph saying all sorts of terrible things. I don't actually think he *will*; he's a kind, good man. But he'll have doubts—who wouldn't? He might even want to break our betrothal contract. He probably won't make a big scene. But even if he doesn't, would I still be welcome in my father's house? Me, the daughter who got mysteriously pregnant? How would my baby and I get by on our own?

So, yes, sometimes I'm scared. All this should have me shaking like King Saul's armies when they faced Goliath—but it just *doesn't*. Because this baby... this life being knit together inside me... he's not going to be ordinary. I don't understand everything his birth will mean, but I know it means this: God is about to do something. Something big. *Really* big!

That helps me a lot when I get scared—remembering God is up to something!

It's why I said yes when the angel told me the news. My baby will be holy, he said. A great king, like David—even greater, in fact, because he'll rule God's people forever! And the angel said God was *honoring* me by choosing me to be this baby's mother. He said God was looking on me with favor.

Imagine that. Me! There's nothing special about me. I'm an ordinary girl, living an ordinary life (well, it *was* ordinary) in the nowhere-special town of Nazareth. I'm no prophet Miriam, even if we do have the same name. I'm no Queen Esther, with influence over the high and mighty. I'm not a leader like Deborah; nobody's calling me "a mother of Israel."

But when I got here, Elizabeth *did* call me the mother of her Lord. She said her baby—*her* miracle baby, given to her in her old age like God gave Isaac to Sarah—was jumping for joy in her belly. And I realized my baby's birth *is* a reason for joy.

If God is looking on someone like me with favor—someone who's really no different from anyone else and who's definitely not perfect; someone who's poor and usually pushed to the side by people who've got money and power; someone who's just trying to love God and my neighbor as best I can—then God really is gracious.

If God is looking on me with favor, then God is looking on all Israel with favor, remembering his promises and getting ready to keep them. God is about to save us. That's why the angel told me to name the baby "Jesus."

No, I'm not scared nearly as much as I should be! Because even though the angel said *I* was the one full of grace, I know the truth.

God is.

Reading for Reflection

Do You Think You're Special?

In 2012, David McCullough, Jr., an English teacher at Wellesley High School in Massachusetts, gave a graduation speech that grabbed public attention as few graduation speeches have. "You are not special," Mr. McCullough told the cap-and-gowned seniors in front of proud parents, family members, and friends. "You are not exceptional. Contrary to what your U9 soccer trophy suggests, your glowing seventh grade report card, despite every assurance of a certain corpulent purple dinosaur, that nice Mister Rogers and your batty Aunt Sylvia, no matter how often your maternal caped crusader has swooped in to save you ... you're nothing special."[1]

If a graduation speaker at your school said that, how would you react?

Mr. McCullough meant his speech as a call "to do whatever you do for no reason other than you love it and believe in its importance." He thinks modern American society is addicted to accolades—an addiction that leads lots of well-meaning adults to force unhealthy expectations of greatness on young people.

The speech went viral; it made headlines across the U.S. and overseas, and it racked up more than a million views on YouTube in under a month. But it attracted so much attention partly because some people—some *adults*—misunderstood it! They heard it as a truth-teller giving a much-needed reality check to a generation of (supposedly) stupendously spoiled, infinitely indulged youth who'd been spoon-fed too much talk of self-esteem.

As he stressed in several interviews, that wasn't Mr. McCullough's intended message. "While they're special to me beyond expression," he wrote in *Newsweek*, "I recognize my kids—like my students—are no more or less important than anyone else's, no more or less deserving of ... lives that matter beyond themselves."[2]

Was Mary "Special"?

I wonder what Mary, the mother of Jesus, would have said had someone told her, "You're not special."

She might have agreed!

That claim may sound strange. After all, isn't the point of this week's Scripture that Mary was *super* special? The archangel Gabriel—who stands in the very presence of God (Luke 1:19) and is entrusted with knowledge of the future (Daniel 8:17)—doesn't show up at just anyone's door with messages from heaven! And *what* a message: "Rejoice, favored one! The Lord is with you!...God is honoring you" (Luke 1:28, 30). Then, when Mary visits her relative Elizabeth, Elizabeth tells her, "God has blessed you above all women..." (1:42). So, based on these verses, couldn't we sing, "Mary's special, this we know, for the Bible tells us so"?

Certainly centuries of art, from ancient mosaics to present-day Christmas cards, give all kinds of visual cues that Mary is special. She's usually beautiful—flawless complexion, delicate features—and looks so serene. She's often dressed in vibrant, richly textured fabrics—*très* stylish. Sometimes the halo around her head is so bright you want to wear shades.

But let's remember some facts about Mary's situation. She is betrothed to Joseph—more binding than a modern engagement, a betrothal was a solemn contract in which a man and woman were already considered married, even before their wedding night—and, in the Judaism of Mary's day, girls got betrothed around age twelve to fourteen. We know she was poor (remember that pair of pigeons she and Joseph sacrifice in Luke 2:24). Calling Nazareth, her home town, "a city in Galilee" (Luke 1:26) is generous: it was a little village of two thousand people, tops.

Was Mary really that special? Not by the world's standards, then or now. She was one poor girl among many poor people. Hopefully, Mary's parents were good parents and thought their daughter was special simply because she was theirs. More than likely, though, nothing marked Mary as special in any way that mattered to the world.

But a big part of the meaning of Christmas is that it's *precisely* the people who don't matter to the world who matter the most to God.

Special to the God Who Saves

The world has always been too addicted to accolades, too easily impressed with credentials, too awestruck by overachievers. But "God doesn't look at things like humans do," as Jesus' ancestor (through adoptive dad Joseph) King David found out (1 Samuel 16:7). The God of Israel has always befriended those overlooked by the world.

Mary sings about this truth when she visits Elizabeth. God champions the lowly and hungry (Luke 1:52-53), people who are without privilege and power, who cry to God for help because they have no one else. God comes to their aid, "remembering his mercy" (1:54). God calls them not just special but "blessed," those who are rejected by others as they hunger and weep in poverty (6:20-21). God promises a radical reversal of fortune to those whom Mary's child would grow up to identify as "the least of these who are members of my family" (Matthew 25:40 NRSV).

Mary answered yes to God's miraculous plan for Jesus' birth, freely naming herself God's servant (Luke 1:38). Maybe she did so with head meekly bowed, as many paintings and Christmas carols would have us believe. But maybe she gave a wholehearted, rousing cheer! After all, she sings, "In the depths of who I am, I rejoice in God my savior" (1:47). Mary was humble, sure, but that doesn't necessarily mean she was quiet! God was sending God's people her baby to be their Savior! That's what the Hebrew name Yeshua—Jesus—means: "God saves." If that's not reason to get excited, what is?

So, no, Mary probably didn't think she was "special." She wasn't full of herself. But that meant she was able to make plenty of room for God. God told her, and all like her, that they, too, were no more or less important than anyone else, no more or less deserving of lives that matter beyond themselves. You can't get more special than mattering to God!

"God stands against the proud, but he gives favor to the humble" (1 Peter 5:5). When you're looking for Christ this Christmas, don't look first to those who are "special" or "exceptional" or "great" as the world sees things. Look for him in humble lives and humble circumstances, because that is where you most likely will see him.

Third pillar with stories from the New Testament: "The Annunciation," Duomo, Orvieto, Italy
(For a full-color image, visit Shutterstock.com and search for 94669597)

Meditating with Art

This sculpture of the Annunciation appears on a pillar in the façade of the cathedral (*duomo*) in Orvieto, Italy. Constructed mostly in the fourteenth century, the cathedral is considered one of the finest if not the finest example of Gothic architecture in Italy.

Two common artistic elements of Annunciation scenes appear in this sculpture. First, Gabriel's staff (a symbol of royal authority) is topped by a fleur-de-lis, or a stylized lily. The lily is associated with Mary as a symbol of her purity. Second, Mary is holding a book. Annunciation scenes often depict her reading or praying with a book (frequently Isaiah's prophecies of the Messiah).

Meditating with Music

Option A. "The Angel Gabriel from Heaven Came" (text by Victorian English hymn-writer Sabine Baring-Gould, based on a traditional hymn from the Basque region in northern Spain)

- What words, phrases, or images from this hymn grab your attention? Write them here. Try using these words as part of your prayers this week.
- How does this hymn influence what you think and feel about the Annunciation?

Option B. Over the centuries, many composers have set the Magnificat—Mary's song of praise in Luke 1:46-55, so called after its first word in Latin—to music. Johann Sebastian Bach's setting (*Magnificat in D major*, BWV 243) is one of the most famous, but there are settings from medieval chant to contemporary Christian music to choose from.

Listen to two settings or songs based on the Magnificat, preferably different in style. On separate pieces of paper, write down or draw the thoughts and feelings each one prompts about Mary, the birth of her son, and the promises of God.

Lectio Divina
Luke 1:46-55

Mary said,

"With all my heart I glorify the Lord!
In the depths of who I am I rejoice in God my savior.
He has looked with favor on the low status of his servant.
Look! From now on, everyone will consider me highly favored because the mighty one has done great things for me.
Holy is his name.
He shows mercy to everyone, from one generation to the next, who honors him as God.
He has shown strength with his arm.
He has scattered those with arrogant thoughts and proud inclinations.
He has pulled the powerful down from their thrones and lifted up the lowly.
He has filled the hungry with good things and sent the rich away empty-handed.

He has come to the aid of his servant Israel, remembering his mercy, just as he promised to our ancestors, to Abraham and to Abraham's descendants forever."

Ponder Giving This Present:
The Heifer Project

Mary's song of praise thanks God for lifting up those who are lowly and filling those who are hungry with good things. Heifer International is dedicated to those goals. It was founded by Dan West, a member of the Church of the Brethren who served as an aid worker during the Spanish Civil War (1936–1939). According to Heifer's website, West's purpose "was to provide relief, but he soon discovered the meager single cup of milk rationed to the weary refugees once a day was not enough. And then he had a thought: What if they had not a cup, but a cow?" (http://www.heifer.org/about-heifer/index.html).

Today, Heifer helps individuals, families, and whole communities develop the knowledge and resources they need to support themselves and achieve a sustainable living. Its charitable gifts catalog (http://www.heifer.org/gift-catalog/index.html) is full of ideas for gifts that can help end poverty and hunger. This Christmas, why not tell the folks on your gift list that you've donated honeybees in their honor, or a share of a sheep in their name? Why not work together with others in your youth group to raise money to buy a water buffalo? (Heifer has online tools for creating decorative cards to tell recipients what you've given and what difference it makes.) Your Christmas giving can transform the lives of people in poverty today, in anticipation of the great reversal Mary sings about.

This Week, Wonder with God About . . .

Sunday – Psalm 145:14-21

Like Mary, the psalm-singer praises God for faithfulness to those who are humble and in distress. When have you sincerely called out to God for help (v. 18)? What happened? How does God use *you* to answer the sincere prayers of others who are in distress?

Monday – 1 Samuel 2:1-10

Mary's Magnificat echoes a song from earlier in Israel's history, one also sung by a woman who experienced an unexpected pregnancy. Hannah, mother of the prophet Samuel, was shamed in her society for her lack of children; when she conceived her son, she praised God for answering her prayers. Read her song slowly, taking time to reflect on her words. How do you see God giving life and raising up (v. 6) in your own life and in the world around you?

Tuesday – Matthew 1:18-25

Luke tells us how God announced Jesus' birth to Mary. Matthew tells us in his Gospel how God announced Jesus' birth to Joseph. How does Joseph demonstrate humility in his response to the news of Mary's miraculous pregnancy? How do you, like both Joseph and Mary, humbly obey God?

Wednesday – Philippians 2:5-11

Paul may be quoting an early Christian hymn in these verses. If so, since the words are all about Christ's coming to us as one of us, we might think of it as one of the earliest Christmas carols! Read these verses slowly, more than once. How did Jesus embody humility in his life and his death? When do you find it hardest to adopt that same attitude (v. 5)? How does God's exaltation of Jesus help you adopt it?

Thursday – 1 Corinthians 1:26-31

The Apostle Paul, who helped organize early Christian congregations throughout the ancient Mediterranean world, had plenty of firsthand experience seeing how God chose some of the unlikeliest characters— himself included—to demonstrate holy living to the world. How has God's "foolishness" surprised you? How do you "brag in the Lord" (v. 31)?

Friday – Matthew 25:31-46

We don't need to *explain* Jesus' parable of "the sheep and the goats" so much as we need to *live* it, until we are no more aware of the times we've helped Jesus than are the people placed by the king on his right side. How do you make caring for those who are "the least" of Jesus' sisters and brothers a part of your life, not just during the holiday season but all year?

Saturday – Ephesians 2:4-10

These verses contain one of Scripture's most powerful discussions of God's amazing grace. Read them carefully. What is grace, according to this text? What does God's grace objectively do? How do we subjectively feel and experience God's grace in our lives? Why does God show us grace in the first place? What "good things" (v. 10) has God prepared for you to do?

5.

IT WAS NOT A SILENT NIGHT

Lighting the Advent and Christ Candles

The Lord be with you!
And also with you!

The people walking in darkness have seen a great light.
A child is born to us, a son is given to us, and authority will be on his shoulders.
He will be named Wonderful Counselor, Mighty God, Eternal Father, Prince of Peace.
There will be vast authority and endless peace for David's throne and for his kingdom.

—Isaiah 9:2, 6-7b

Scripture Focus
Luke 2:1-7

In those days Caesar Augustus declared that everyone throughout the empire should be enrolled in the tax lists. This first enrollment occurred when Quirinius governed Syria. Everyone went to their own cities to be enrolled. Since Joseph belonged to David's house and family line, he went up from the city of Nazareth in Galilee to David's city, called Bethlehem, in Judea. He went to be enrolled together with Mary, who was promised to him in marriage and who was pregnant. While they were there, the time came for Mary to have her baby. She gave birth to her firstborn child, a son, wrapped him snugly, and laid him in a manger, because there was no place for them in the guestroom.

Mary Ponders

The baby is crying. Again. Jesus is a very *loud* baby. How can such little lungs be so full of sound?

Didn't I just feed you, baby? Can't you let me sleep?

"Mary?"

It's Joseph, speaking softly, gently shaking my shoulder. "He's hungry."

"I *know*." I sit up and groan. I'm sore.

Joseph lifts Jesus from the manger. He handles him clumsily, which makes Jesus cry even louder. Joseph probably doesn't think I see the relief that flashes across his face as he hands the baby over.

I make little shushing sounds at Jesus as I rub his face against my breast. He makes a satisfied little grunt as he latches on and starts to suck.

Joseph watches, a strange look on his face.

"You've never seen a woman nurse a baby before?" I ask—amused, annoyed. And *so* tired.

Joseph says, "I've never seen *my wife* nurse *our* baby before."

I feel tears run down my face. I smile. I don't have words. I pull the baby closer. I'm *exhausted*, and hurting, and have no idea what is going to happen next—but I see this *is* a moment of beauty.

Even if it's not how I'd imagined it.

The angel forgot to tell me the Emperor's census would make Joseph and me temporarily homeless. And the angel never said we'd have to go all the way from Nazareth, where we would have been surrounded by family and friends, to Bethlehem, where *nobody* knows us. *And* the angel hadn't warned us we'd have no place to stay once we got here—after ten days on the road, walking uphill most of the way. The trip would have been hard even if I'd been feeling my best—which I *wasn't*!

And the manger. A *manger*! Putting my baby in a cold, stone feeding trough....I can hardly stand it. I know Jesus will live and die a poor person; Joseph and I can't change that. But no child, *no* child, should have to start life like this. Humility is one thing; this is squalor, and it's shameful. Why won't the rich find room in their homes, in their hearts, not just for my poor child, but for all poor children?

Wait. The baby has stopped nursing. I gasp. Is he all right? I think of the many women I've known in Nazareth whose babies didn't live long at all....

Then Jesus burps.

I can't help but laugh. I look at his face and think again, as I have so many times these last nine months, about what the angel *did* tell me. He said *my* son would be called *God's* son. He said my son would rule God's people forever. He said my son would save us all.

How strange, how marvelous, that God would keep all the ancient promises in this way...that God would send the Savior on whom we helpless sinners will depend as a helpless baby, totally dependent, for now, on *us*. Maybe it's my lack of sleep talking, or the stress of the last few days—of the last nine months—but the thought makes me want to laugh and cry all at the same time: Our salvation is starting right here, right now, with this little lump of a person who's fallen asleep on my chest....

Somewhere nearby, cattle are lowing. My baby awakes.

And, yet again, he starts to cry. (Did I mention he has a very loud cry?)

But I don't mind. I hold him close, rocking him, soothing him. Cry all you want, Jesus, as loud as you like; I might even join you. Our God knows we have plenty to cry about in this world, especially people like you and me—the poor, the pushed aside. But our God is here, in *you*, baby, crying right along with us…and promising that one day, through you, all the crying will stop, and all our tears will be wiped away.

The louder Jesus cries, the louder the cattle low. And Joseph is talking—arguing?—with some people who've shown up out of nowhere…are they shepherds, babbling loudly about angels? (They must be; they smell like shepherds.) No one's going to be sleeping in peace around here tonight—and tomorrow we'll be on the move, starting the long slog back to Nazareth.

But my God has come to me—God has come to us all—and will be making the journey with us. And as I hold Jesus and silently bless the Lord, I find in my heart the silent night I crave, a peace beyond any human understanding. I will hang on to it and cherish it and ponder it always, no matter where this baby's life leads him and leads me. I will remember and return to this moment, when I could first see with my eyes and touch with my hands the God who saw and shaped me even before my own birth.

I will witness it all, and give my testimony to whoever will hear: Jesus, the Savior, is born!

Not-So-Silent Night[1]

Silent night? Not tonight!
Angels shout with great might,
"God is doing a marvelous thing! God has sent you the Savior and King!"
Loudly share the good news! Loudly share the good news!

Silent night? Not tonight!
Mary holds Jesus tight,
Newborn baby—much crying he makes—come from heaven for all of our sakes.
Greet Messiah with joy! Greet Messiah with joy!

Silent night? Not tonight!
We must sing of God's light!
Let the world that such darkness has known,
Hear the Word: We are not left alone!
Christ is with us, the Lord! Christ is with us, the Lord!

NOTES

Introduction
1. Beverly Roberts Gaventa, *Mary: Glimpses of the Mother of Jesus* (Columbia, South Carolina: University of South Carolina Press, 1995), page 130.

Session One
1. See http://romania-insights.com/listings/neamt-monastery/ (accessed August 2, 2015).
2. See http://campus.udayton.edu/mary/resources/antiph3.html (accessed August 2, 2015).
3. See http://www.americanbible.org/bible-ministry/areas-of-focus (accessed August 2, 2015).

Session Three
1. Marlise Simons, "Brother Roger, 90, Dies; Ecumenical Leader," *New York Times*, 18 August 2005; http://www.nytimes.com/2005/08/18/world/europe/brother-roger-90-dies-ecumenical-leader.html?_r=0.

Session Four
1. "Wellesley High Grads Told: 'You're Not Special,' " *The Swellesley Report*, June 5, 2012; http://theswellesleyreport.com/2012/06/wellesley-high-grads-told-youre-not-special/.
2. "David McCullough: My Turn on the 'You're Not Special' Speech," *Newsweek*, June 18, 2012; http://www.newsweek.com/david-mccullough-my-turn-youre-not-special-speech-65243.

Session Five
1. *Bible Lessons for Youth*, Winter 2014-15, ISBN 9781426781803, © 2014 by Cokesbury. Used by permission. All rights reserved.

CPSIA information can be obtained at www.ICGtesting.com
Printed in the USA
LVOW07s0525270815

451502LV00004B/5/P